Not in Need of Quests

A Coloring Book of Men in Fantasy Settings

by author/artist
M.C.A. Hogarth

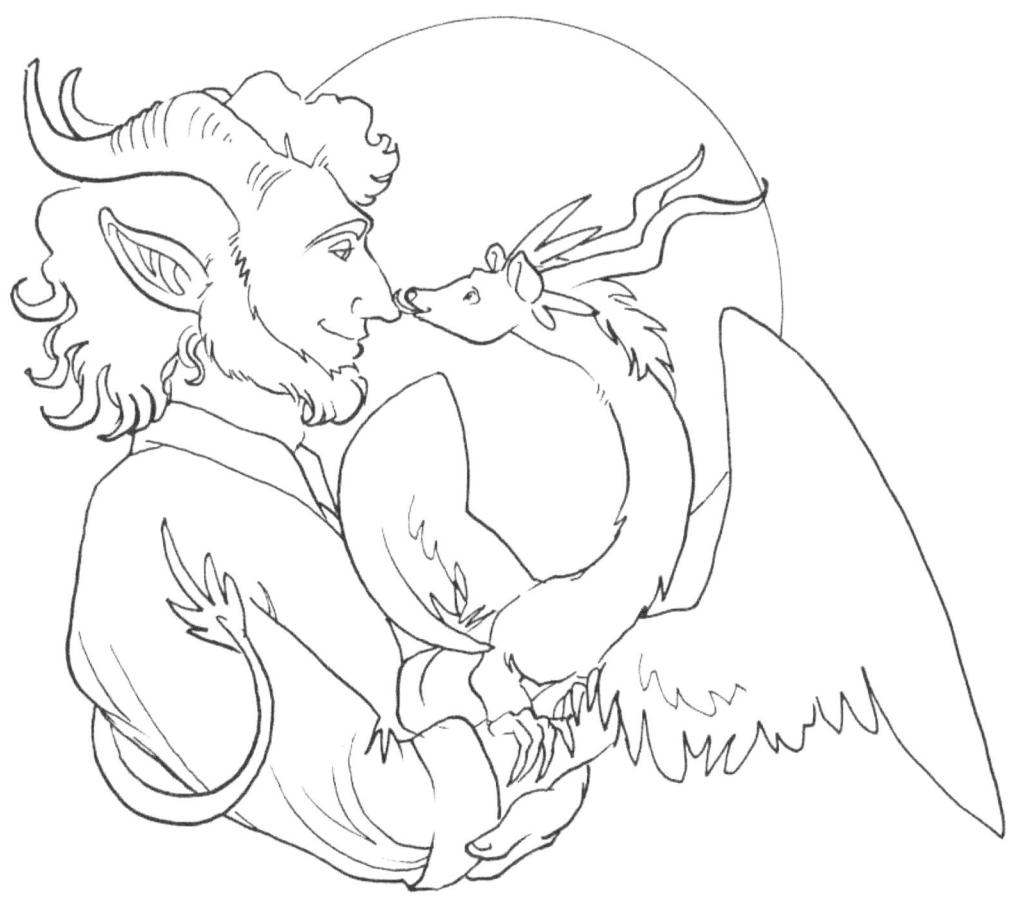

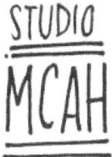

STUDIO
MCAH

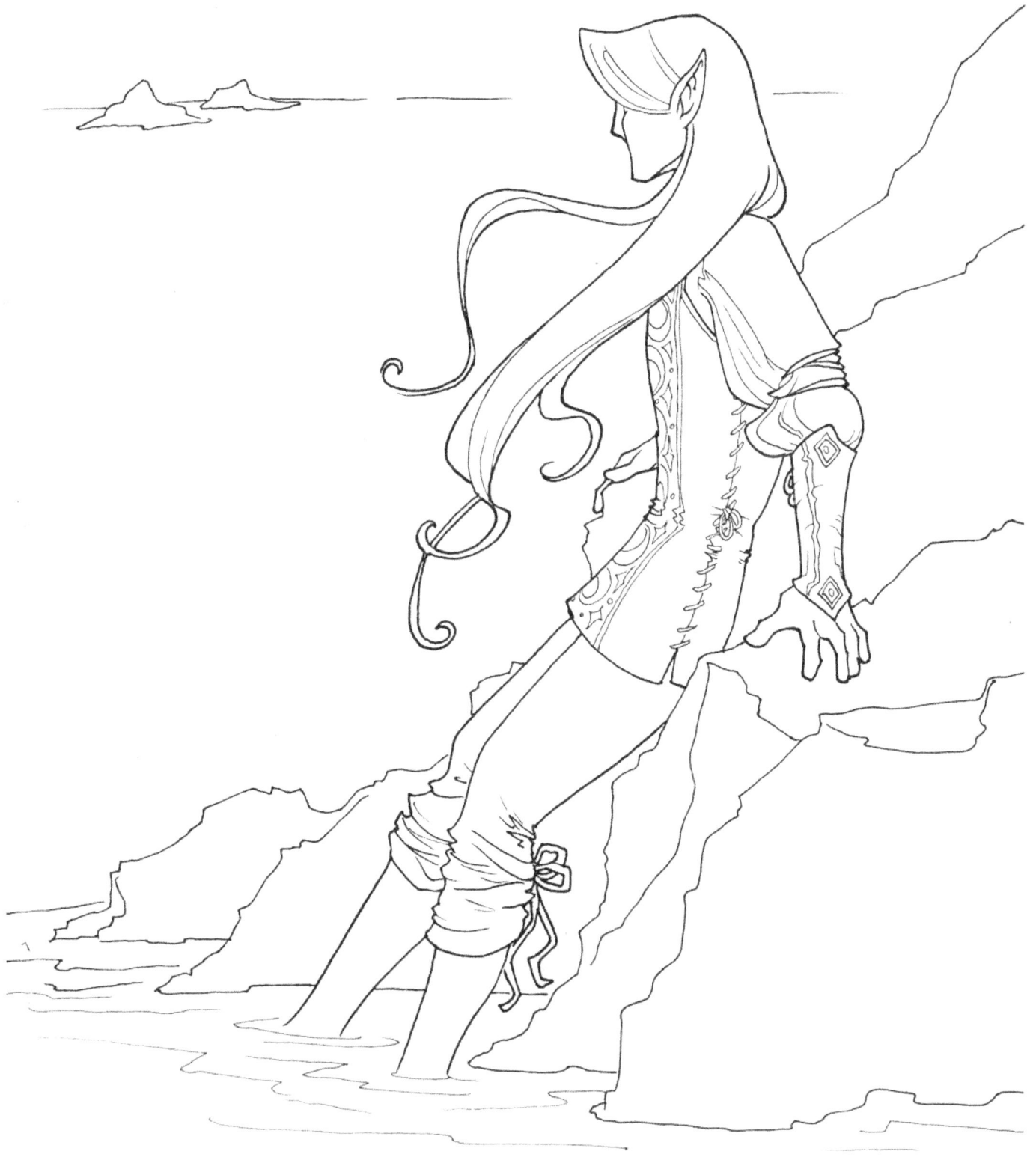

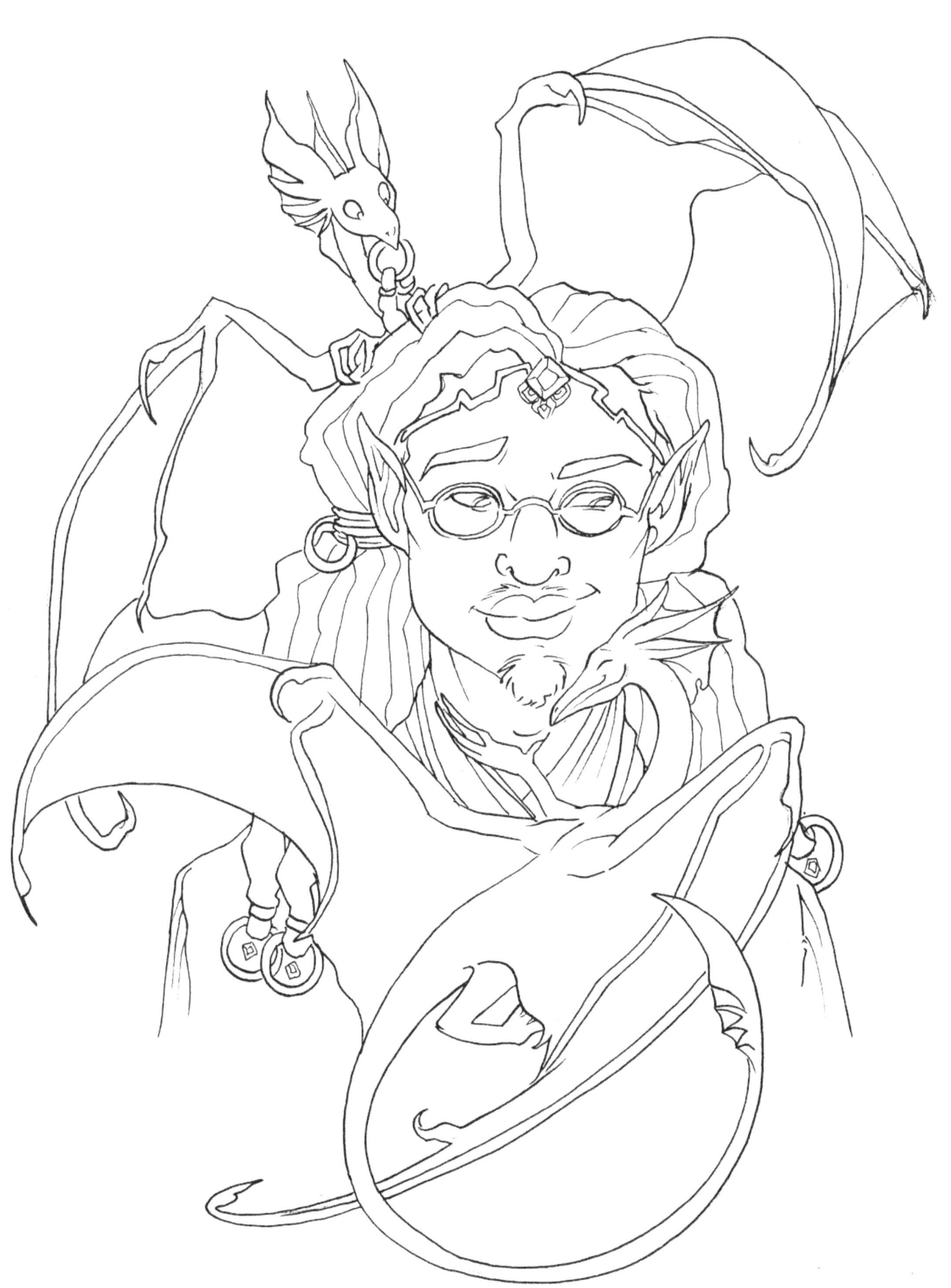

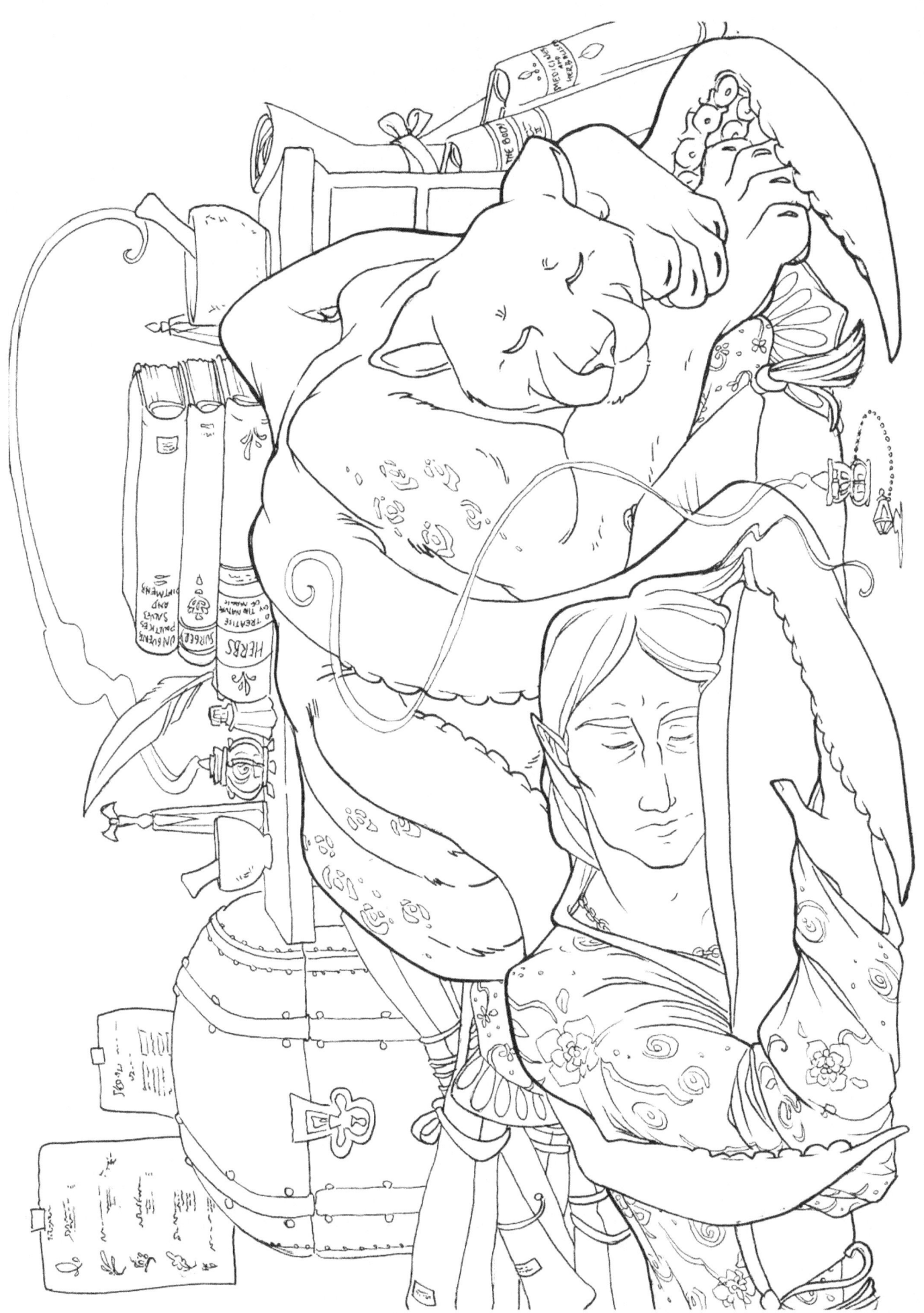

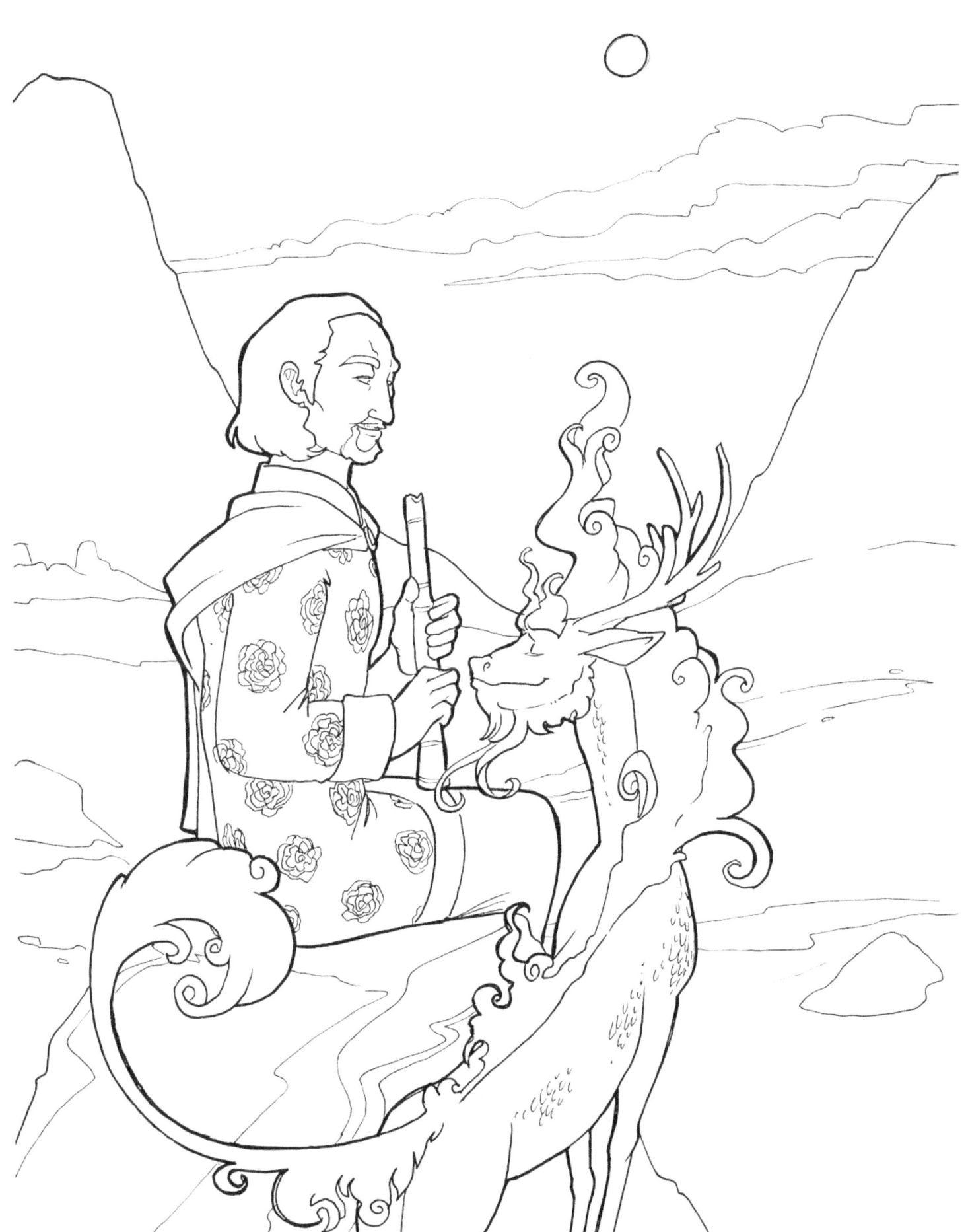

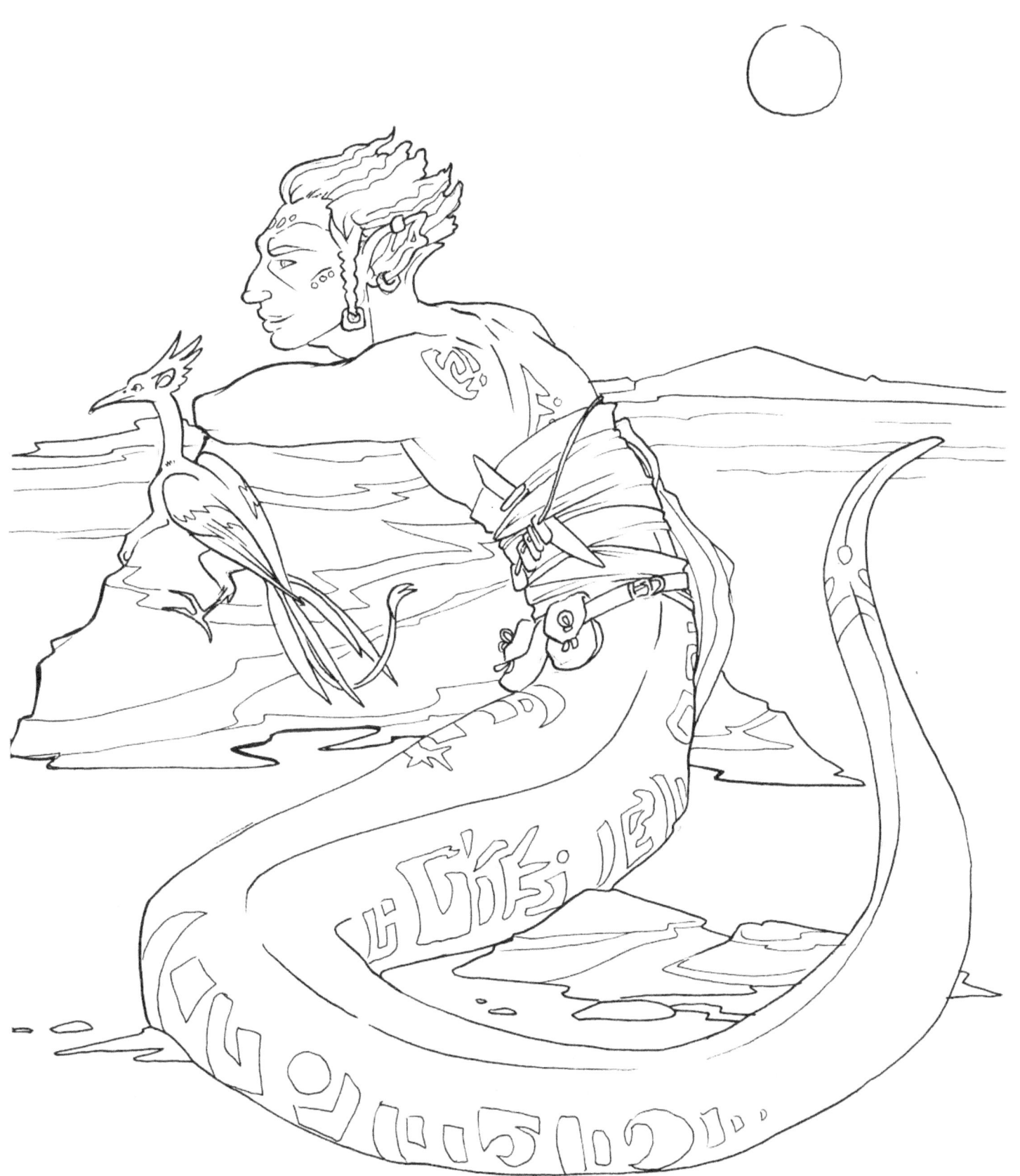

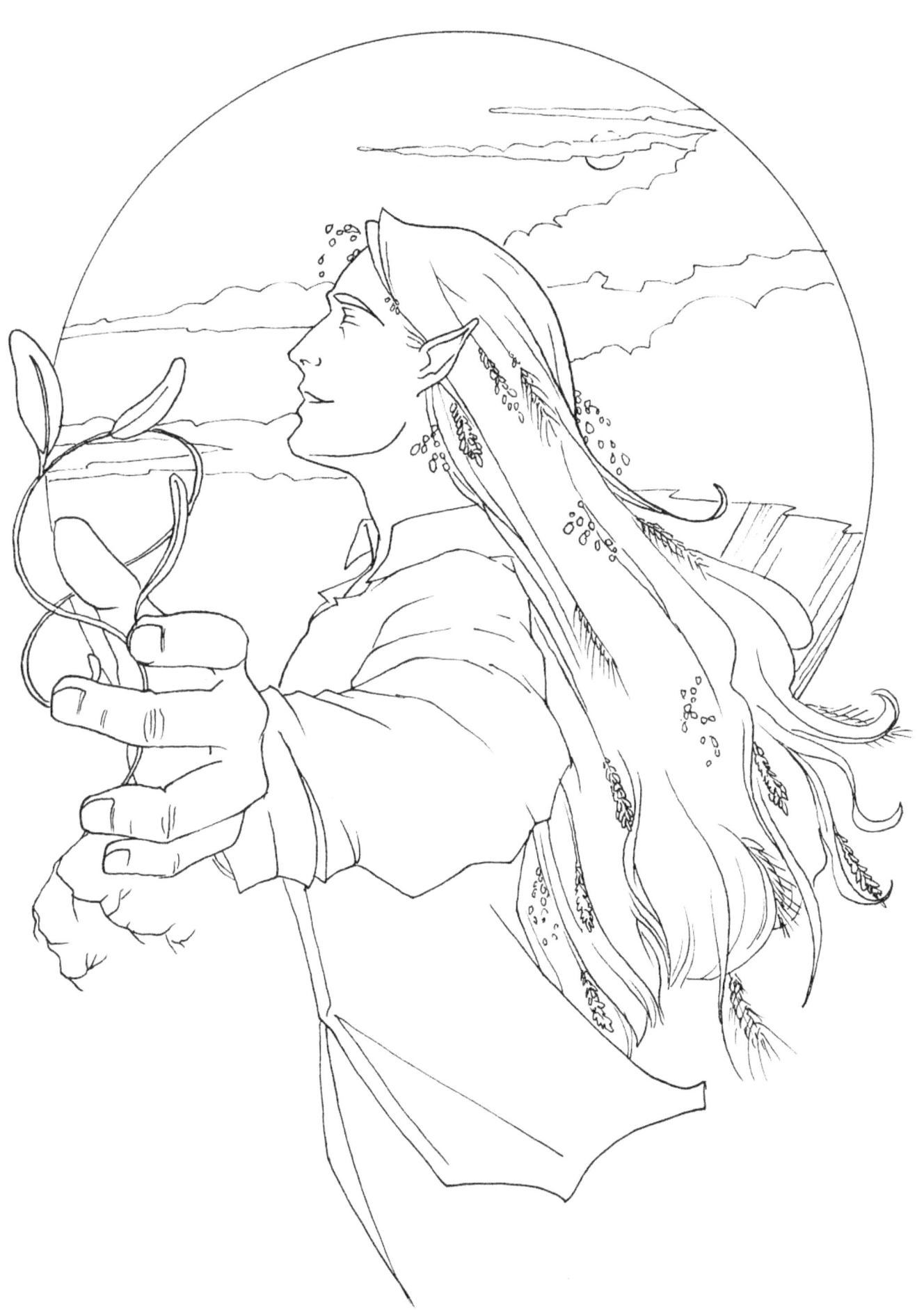

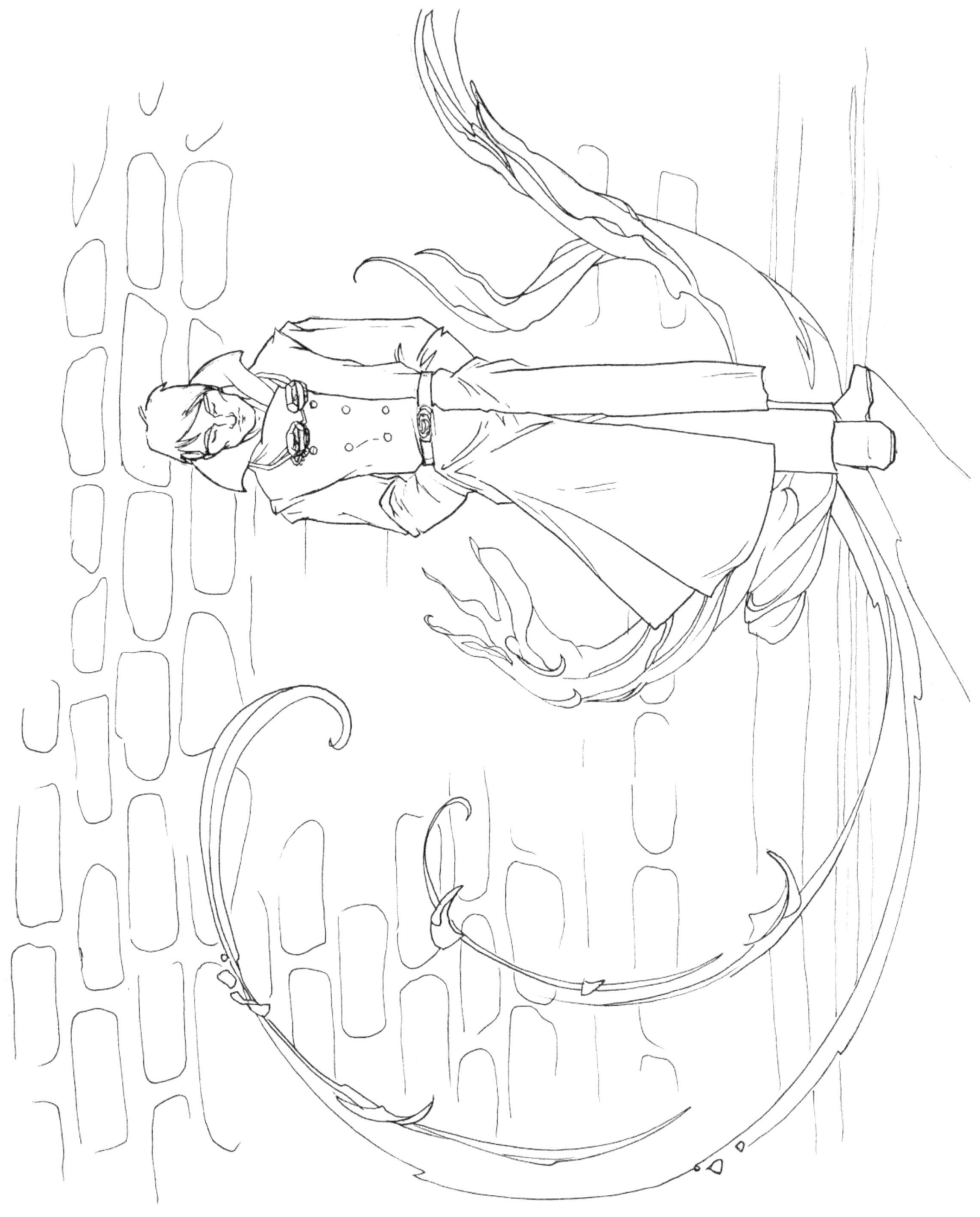

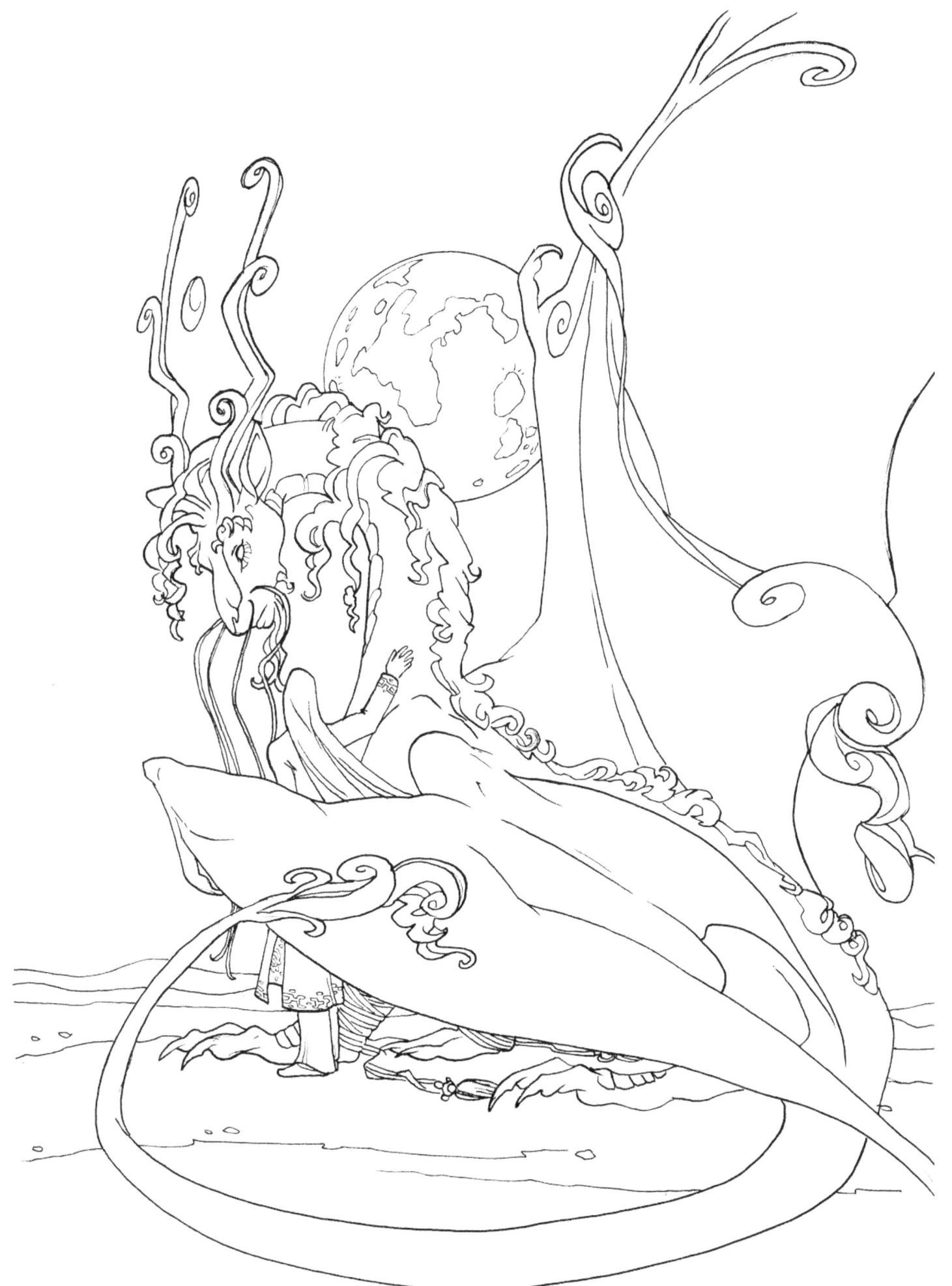

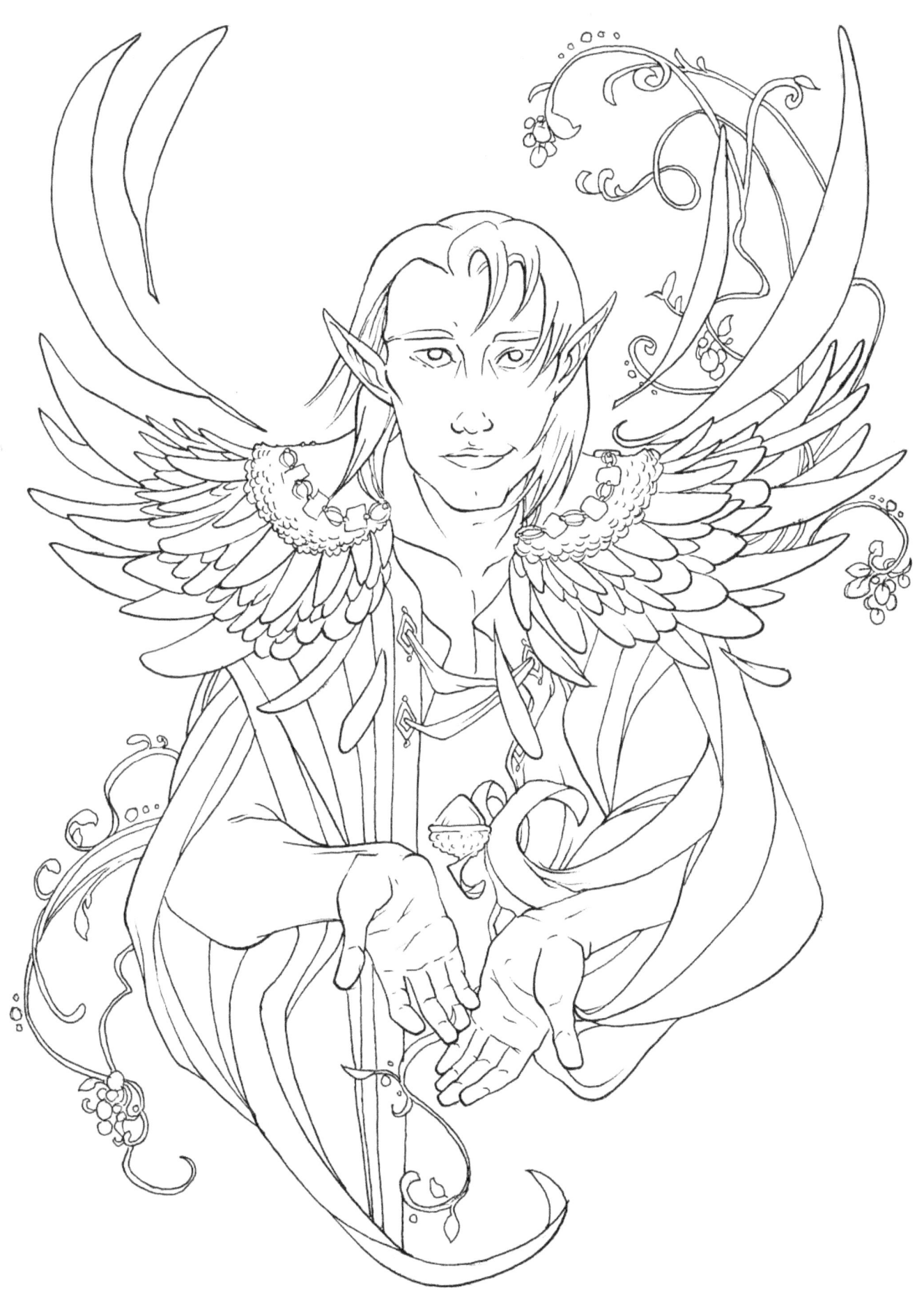

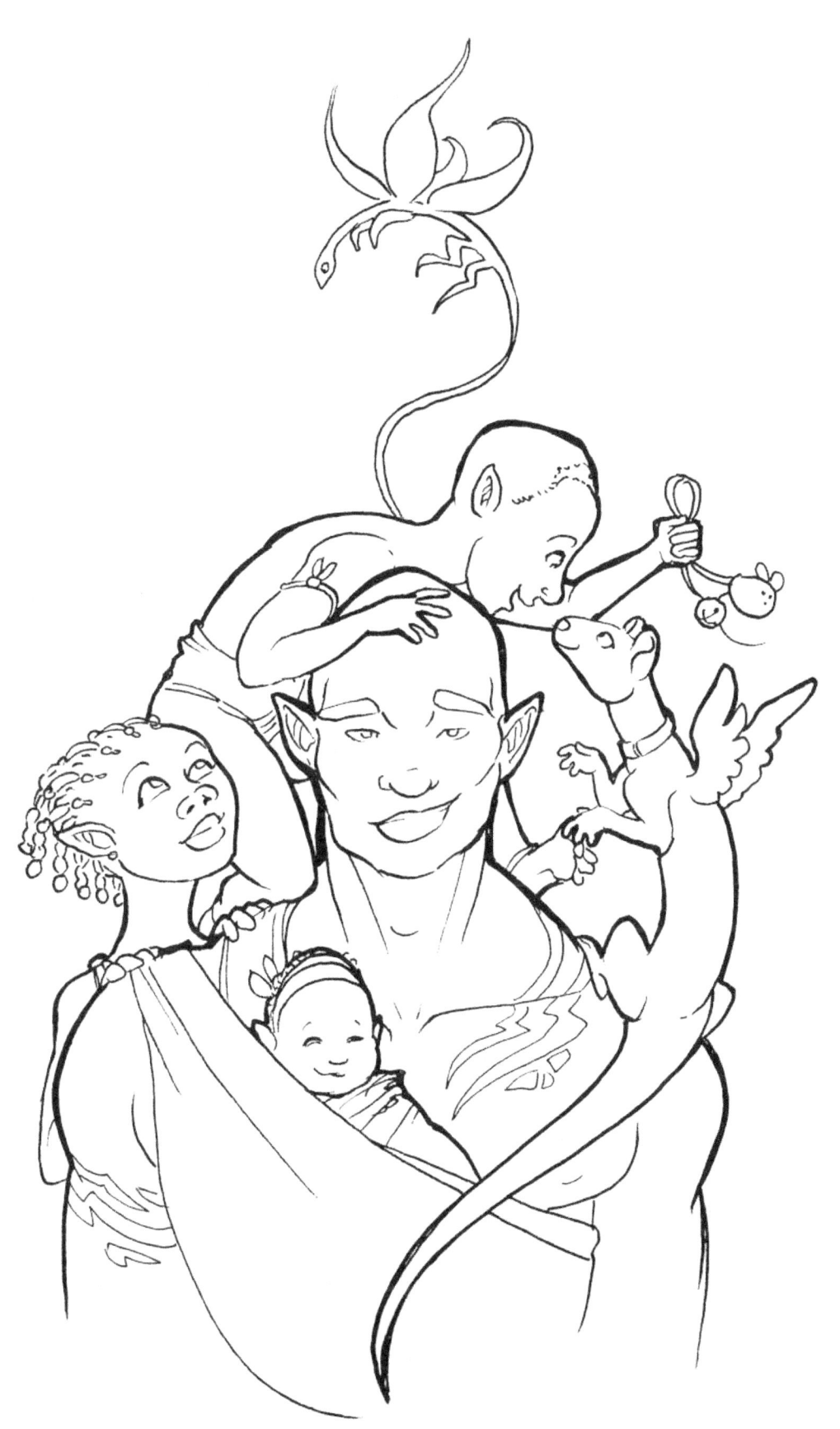

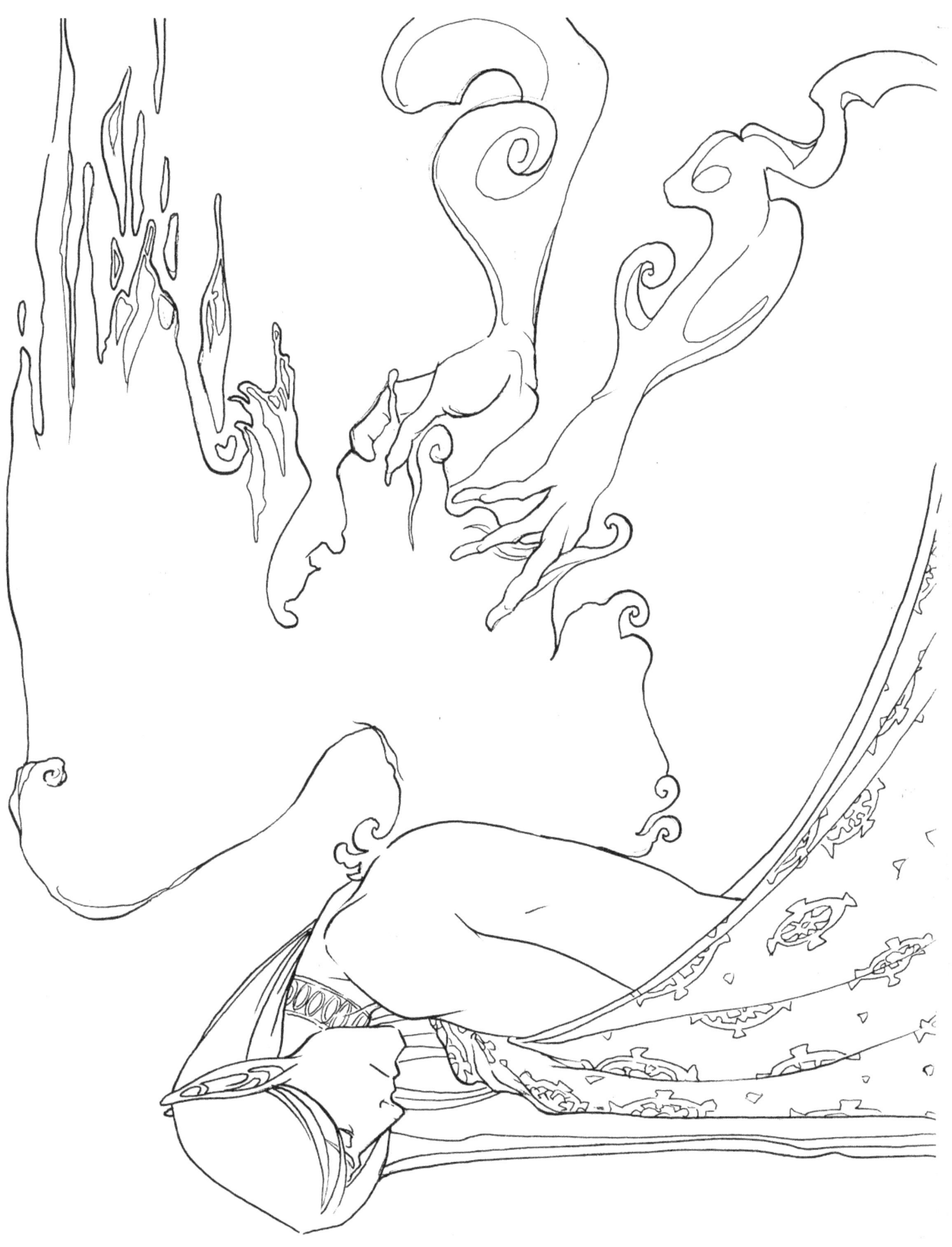

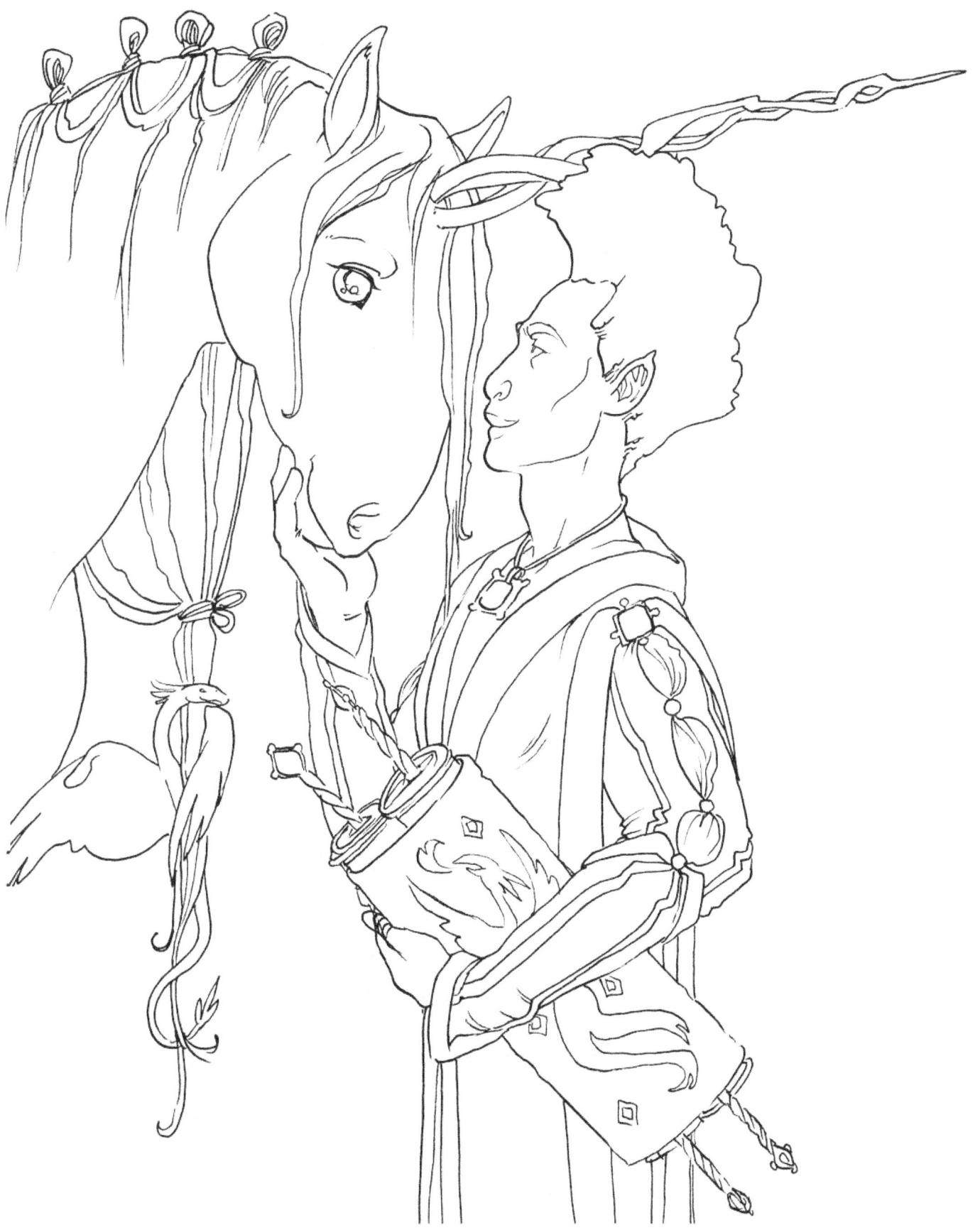

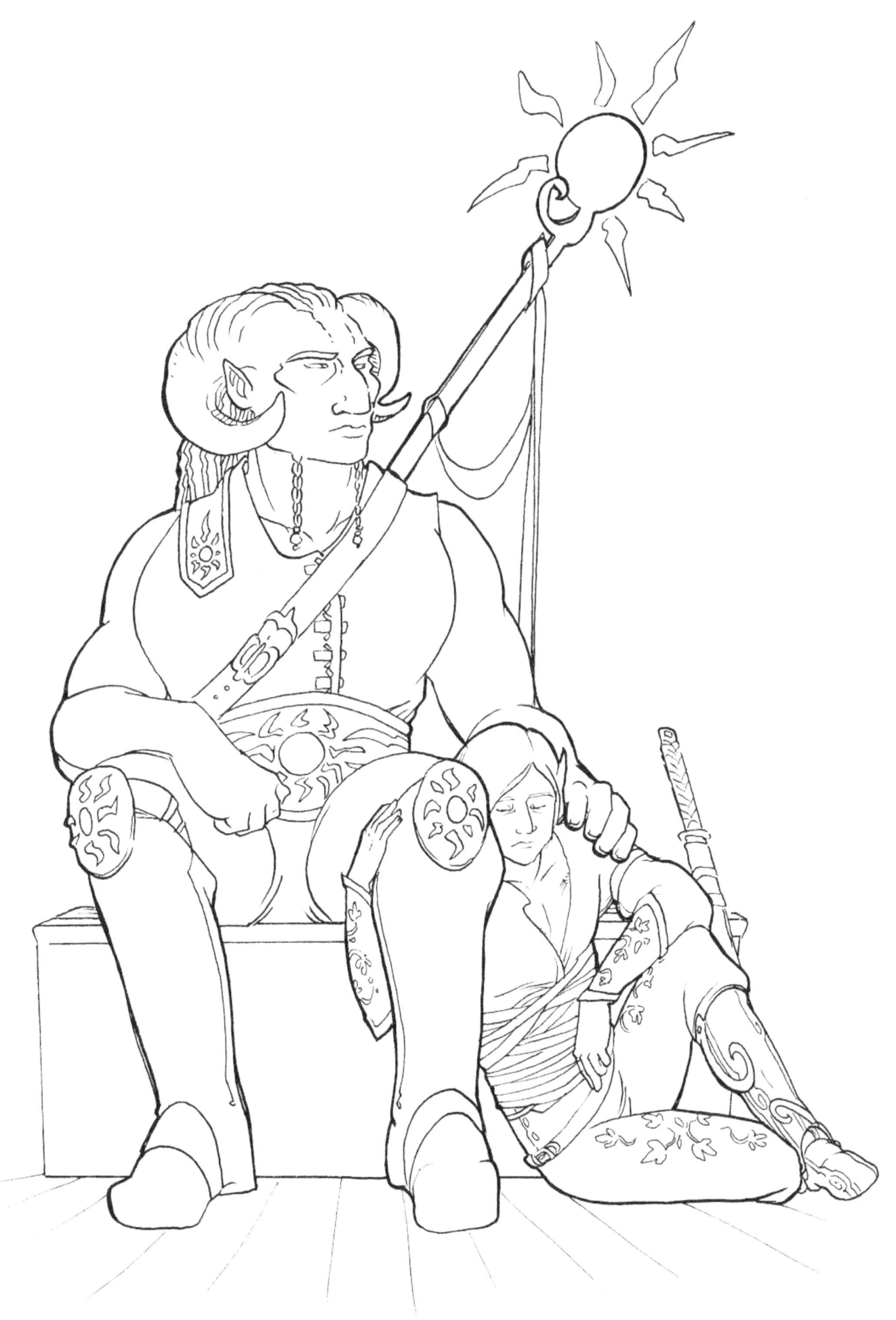

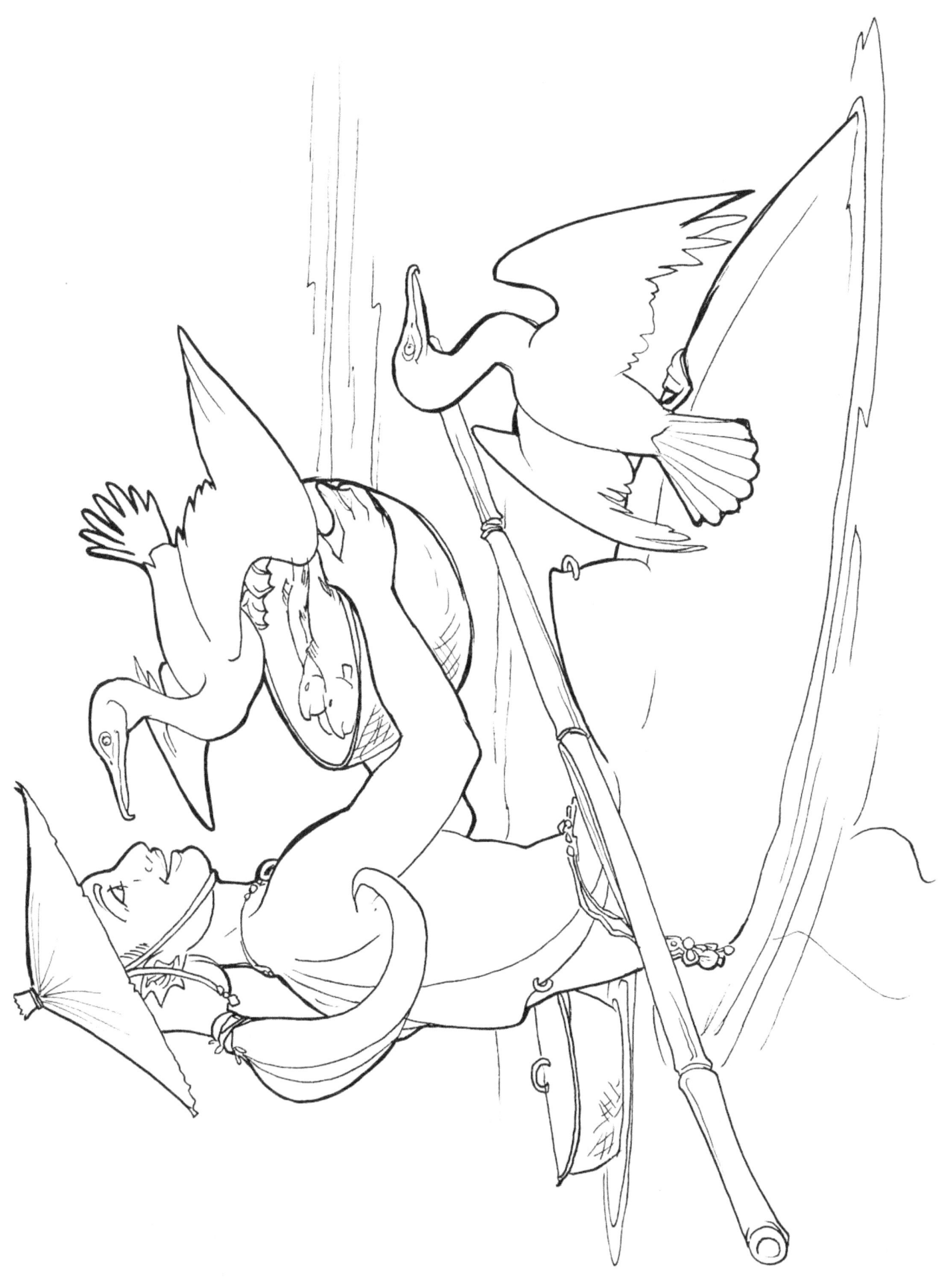

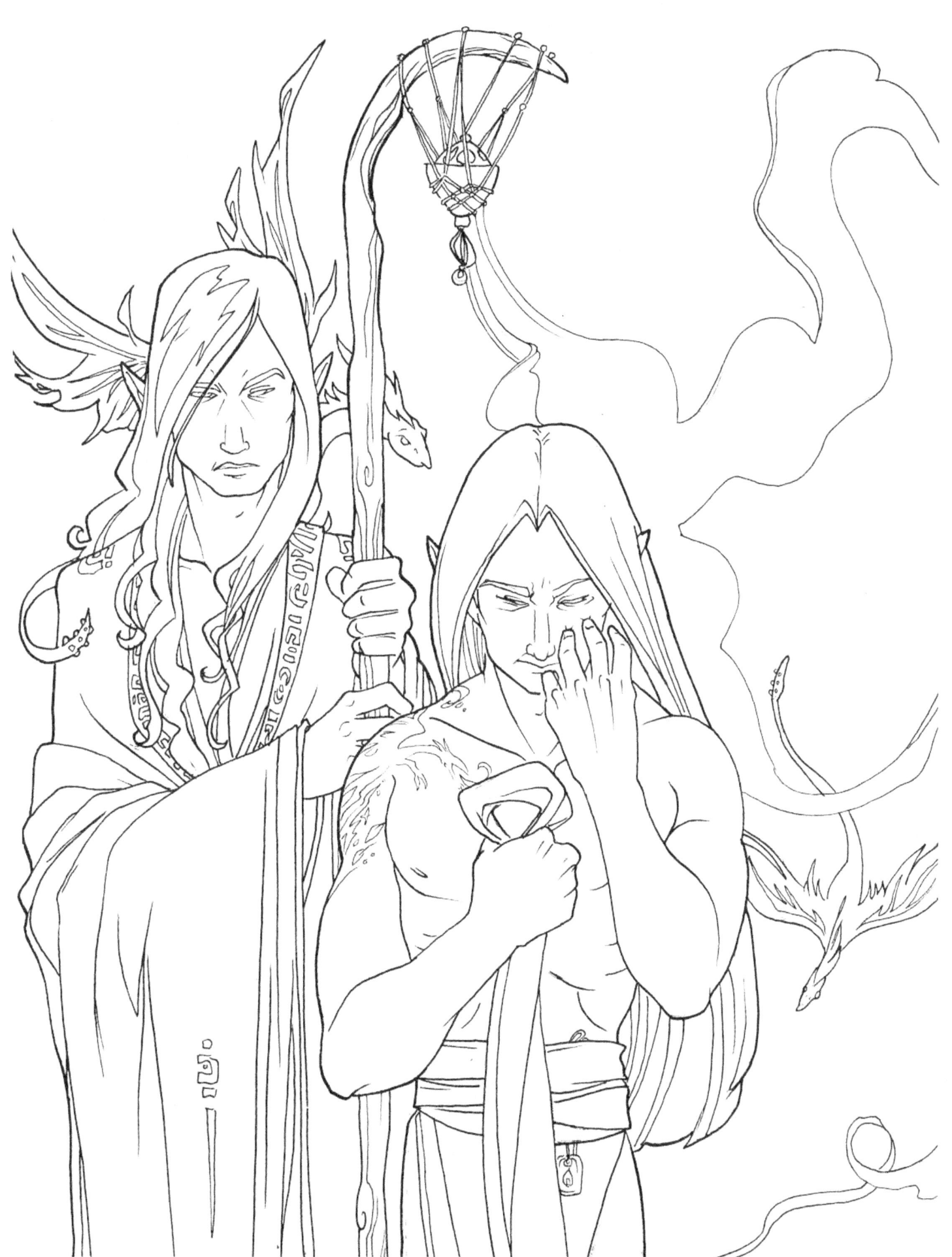

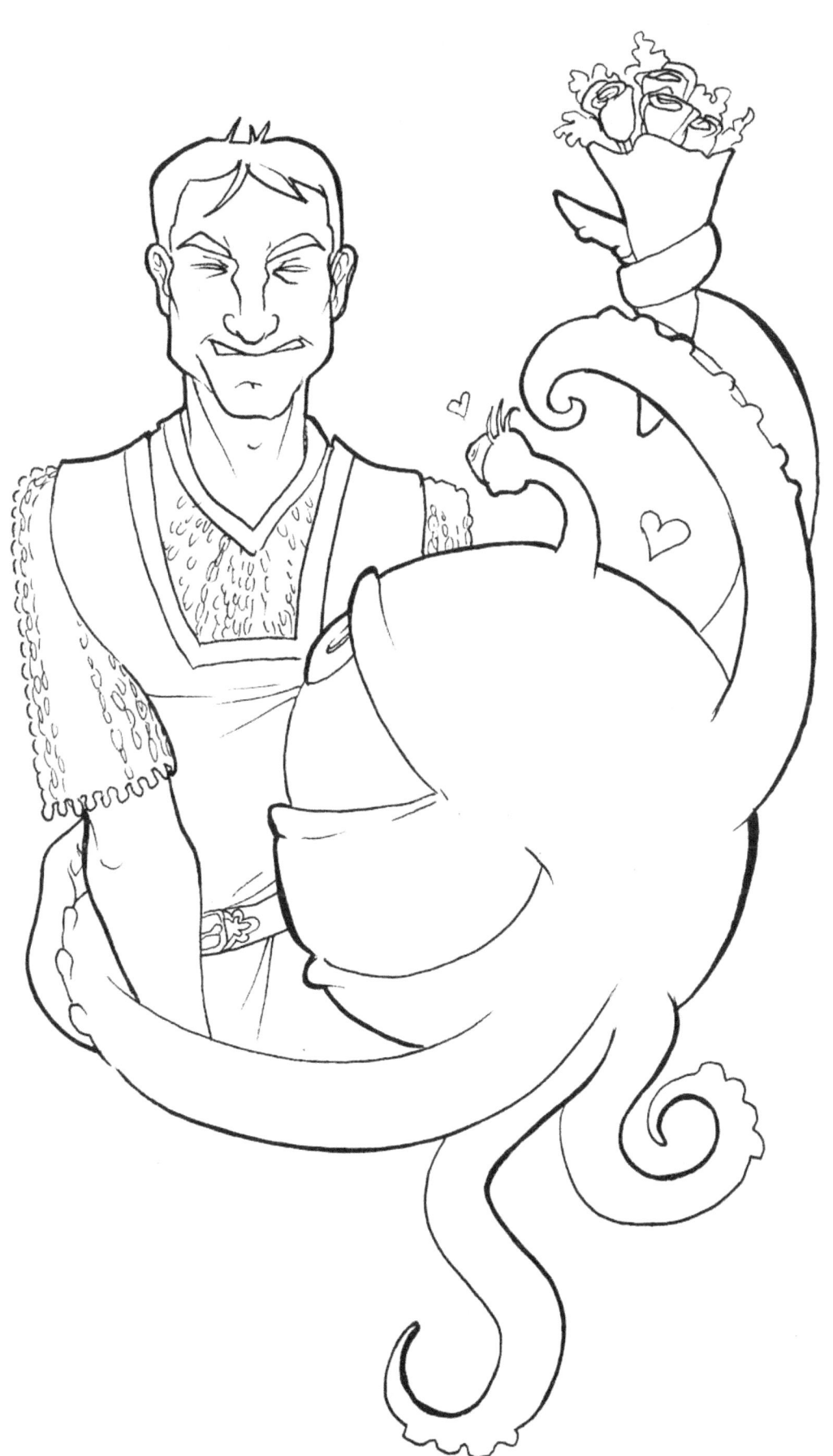

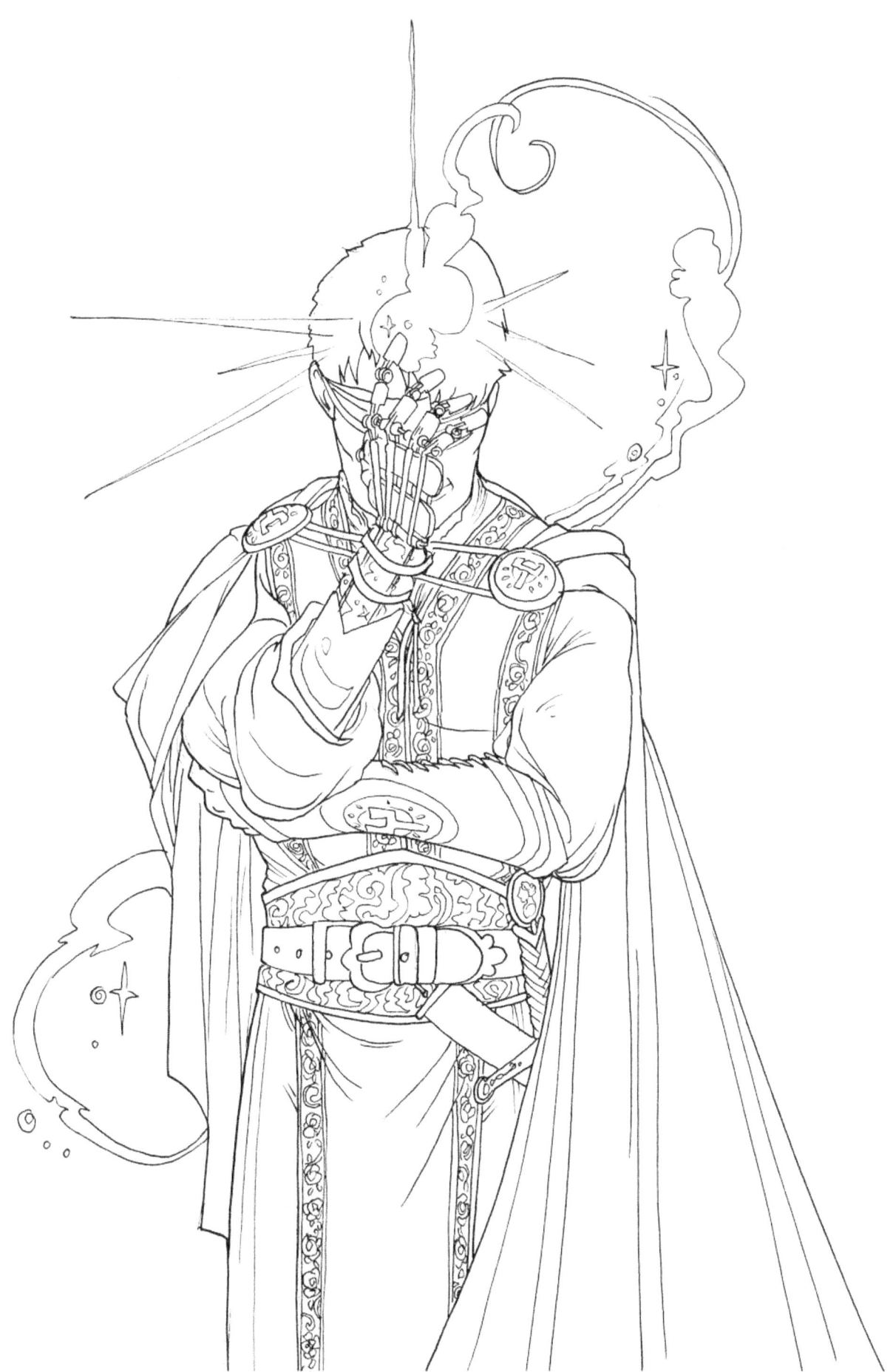

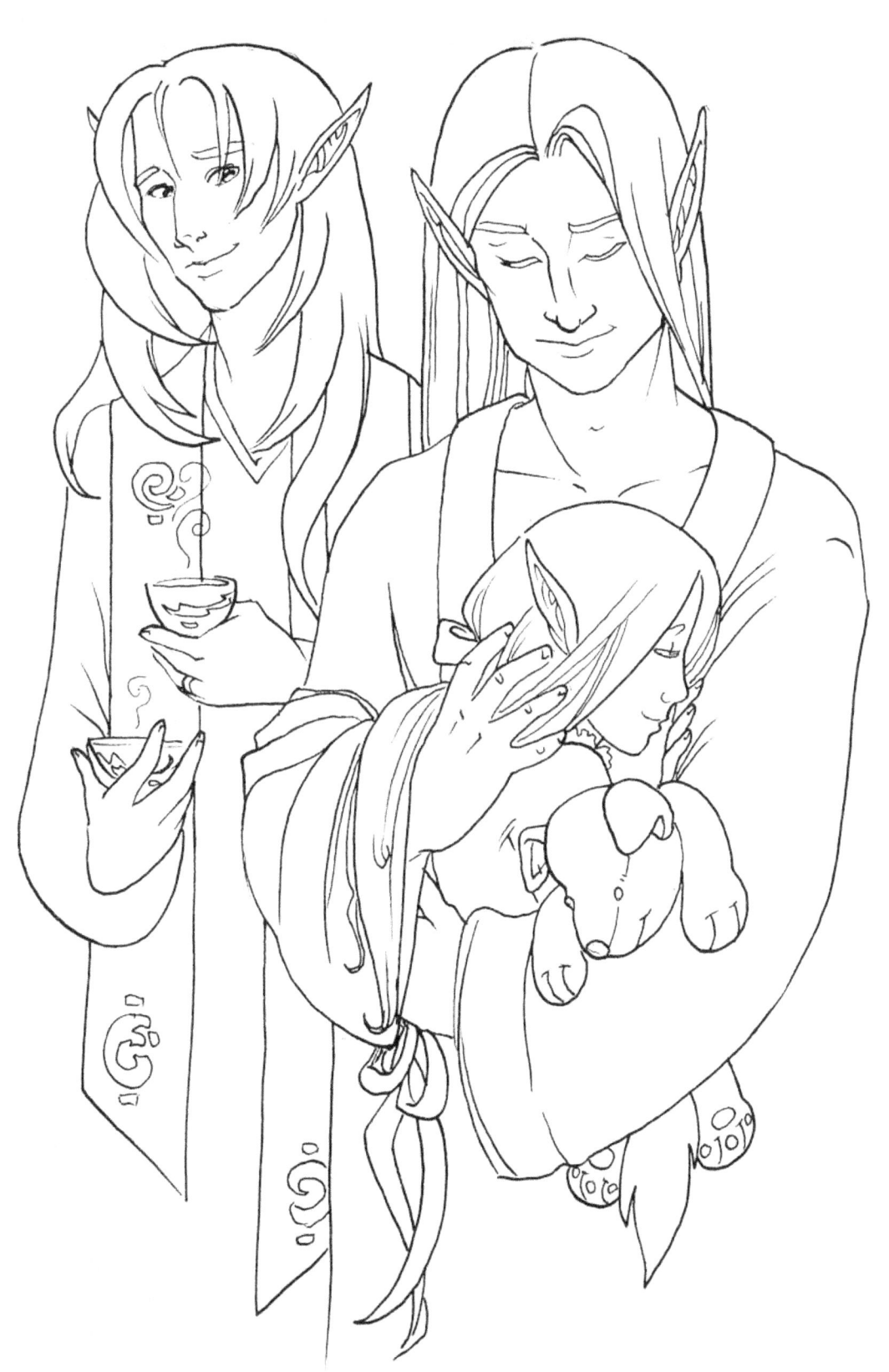

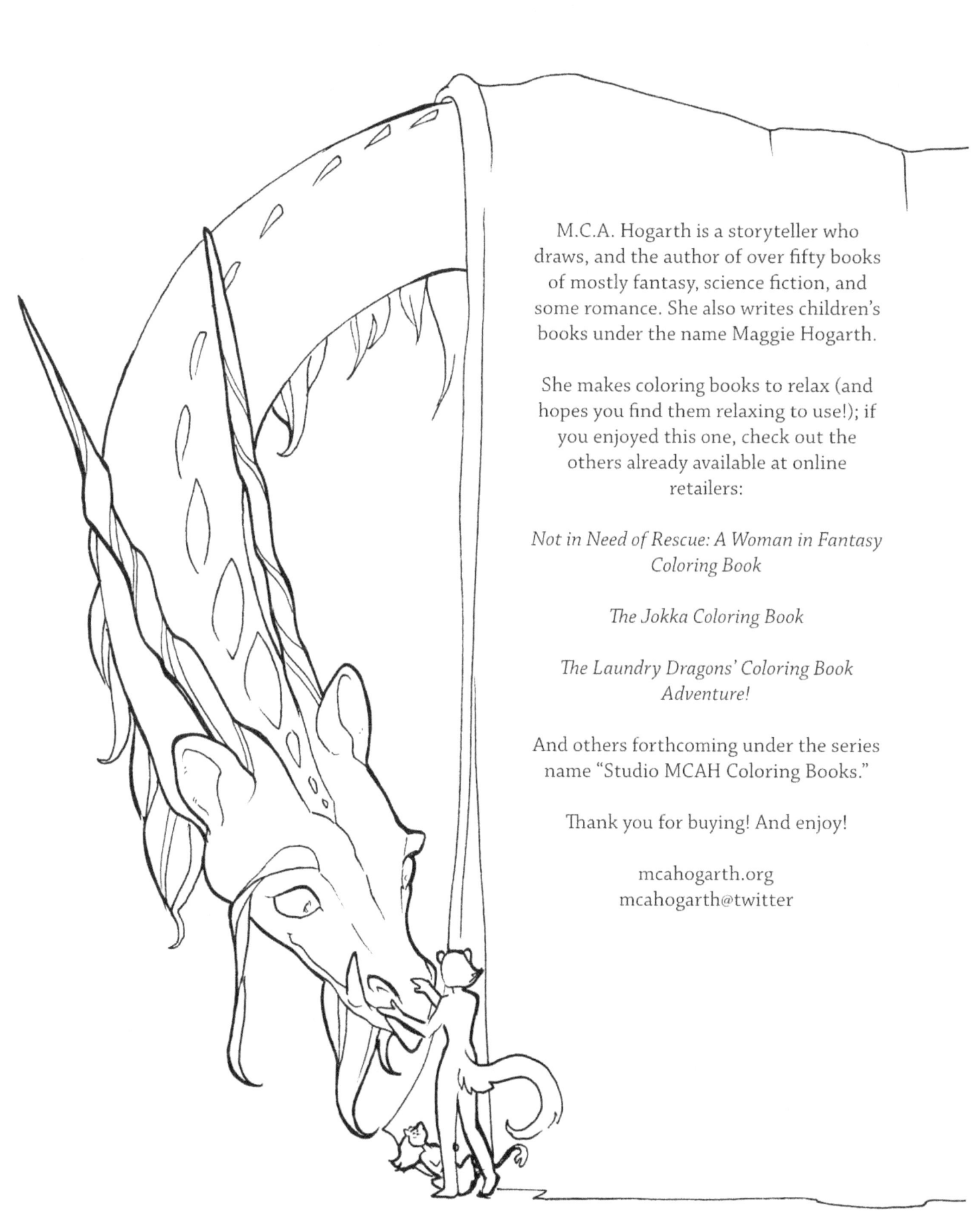

M.C.A. Hogarth is a storyteller who draws, and the author of over fifty books of mostly fantasy, science fiction, and some romance. She also writes children's books under the name Maggie Hogarth.

She makes coloring books to relax (and hopes you find them relaxing to use!); if you enjoyed this one, check out the others already available at online retailers:

Not in Need of Rescue: A Woman in Fantasy Coloring Book

The Jokka Coloring Book

The Laundry Dragons' Coloring Book Adventure!

And others forthcoming under the series name "Studio MCAH Coloring Books."

Thank you for buying! And enjoy!

mcahogarth.org
mcahogarth@twitter

www.ingramcontent.com/pod-product-compliance
Lightning Source LLC
Chambersburg PA
CBHW081241170526
45165CB00009B/3147